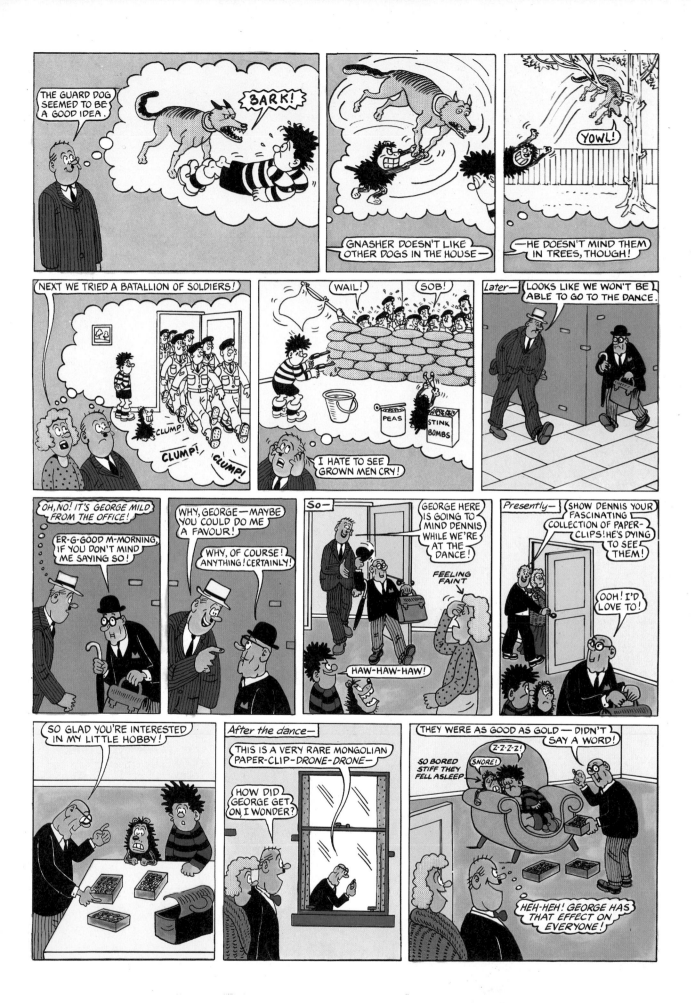

B

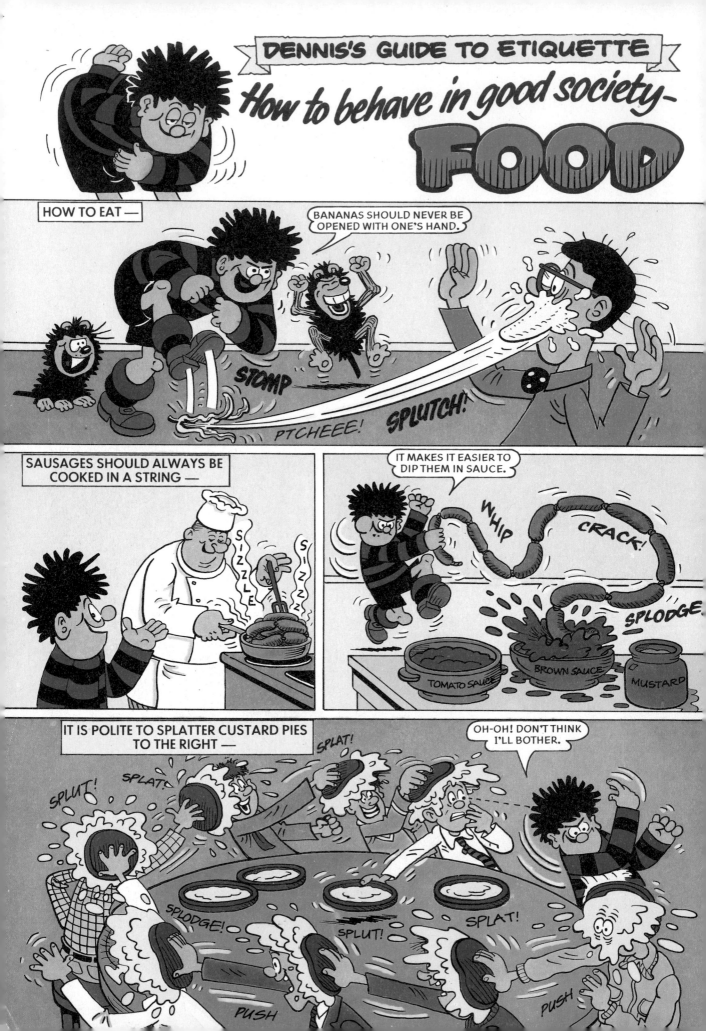

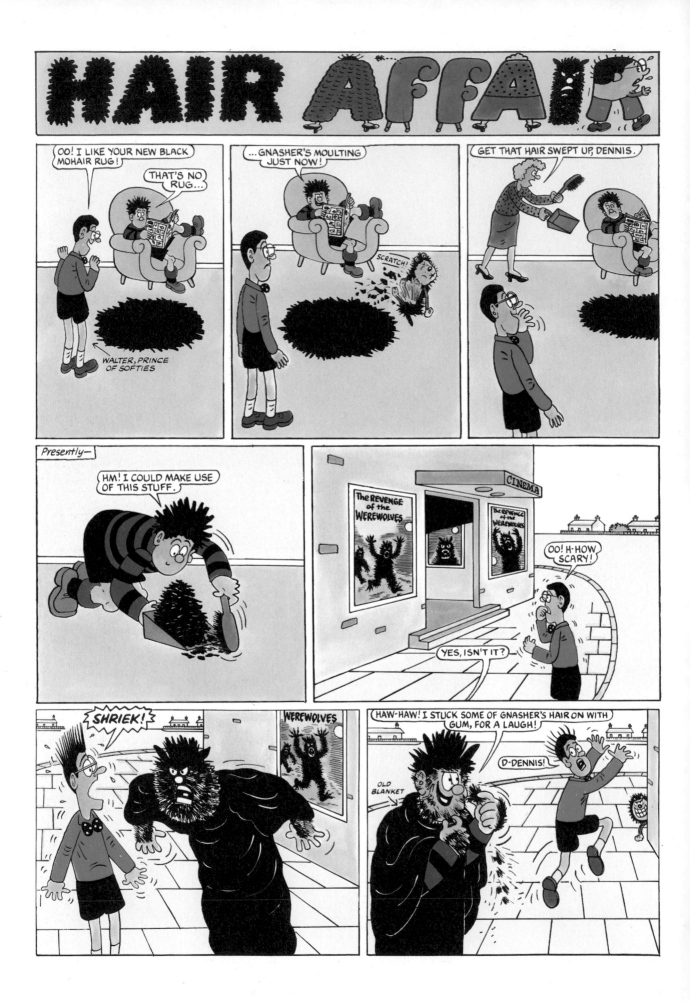

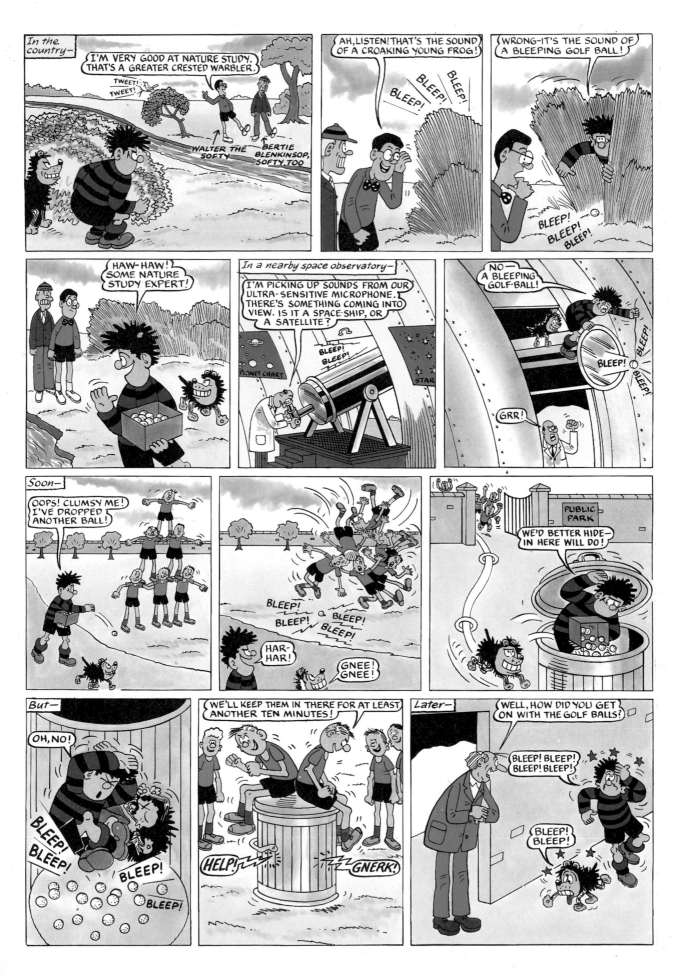

DENNIS'S GRANNY SHOWS SOME
GRANNY'S REMEDIES

The LONG GOODPIE

It had been a quiet day at Dennis's Detective Agency. Mrs Smith from down the road had been in to ask him to find her missing cat, Squidgles. Dennis was not keen on the name, but business is business to a private detective — even if he isn't a real one. Finding the cat had been easy. Getting Gnasher to let it down from the tree had taken a little longer. Dennis thought that getting Mrs Smith to dress up as a giant bone to lure him away had been a good idea. Mrs Smith was not so sure. Still it serves her right for giving her cat such a daft name.

Suddenly the peace was broken. So was almost everything else in Dennis's office — er — Dad's shed. Dennis's pal, Pie Face, ran about the shed screaming and knocking things off shelves. "Stop! Stop! You're turning the place upside down," said Dennis.

"What a good idea," said Pie Face running outside and levering the shed over with a clothes pole.

Dennis crawled from the wreckage to see Pie Face banging his head on the ground in desperation. "Wah! Still can't find any pies. Not a single pie in the whole of Beanotown. Help me, Dennis. I need pies!"

Dennis scratched his chin thoughtfully, then rubbed ointment in his back painfully and put plasters on his head stingingly — it is a bruising business having your office turned upside down. "This sounds like a job for me and my trusty bloodhound, Gnasher. Do you have a picture of one of the missing objects?"

"Yes, I always carry one next to my heart." Pie Face produced a picture of a pie. Dennis showed it to Gnasher before harnessing him up to his cartie. In no time they were heading into town as fast as Gnasher in search of a pie can go — three times as fast as a pea from Dennis's pea shooter — pretty fast.

Dennis dragged them out of the shop. "Let's go. I know where we'll find out what's happened to Beanotown's pie supply. We've got to go to Mr Crusty in Pie Lane."

Pie Face was impressed at the great detective's work. Dennis had actually seen a sign in the shop that said "Our pies are made by Mr Crusty of Pie Lane." They set off for Pie Lane. This time Pie Face was harnessed up and pulling the cartie, Gnasher being too full of pie.

There was still one problem. When they arrived in Pie Lane how would they know where the piemaker lived? There were some clues to go on. Halfway up the street was a large pie-shaped building. Outside it was a sign that read "Mr Crusty's Pie Factory."

They waited and soon the splattered pies spelt out the words "HLEP! I'M BOING KEPT PRISENNIR". This could only mean two things. Someone was keeping Mr Crusty prisoner and it was very difficult to spell out messages by throwing pies across the street on to a wall.

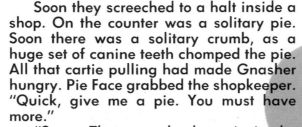

Soon they screeched to a halt inside a shop. On the counter was a solitary pie. Soon there was a solitary crumb, as a huge set of canine teeth chomped the pie. All that cartie pulling had made Gnasher hungry. Pie Face grabbed the shopkeeper. "Quick, give me a pie. You must have more."

"Sorry. That was the last pie in the shop. Our deliveries have stopped completely." Pie Face fell weeping to the floor. Gnasher burped loudly and felt slightly guilty.

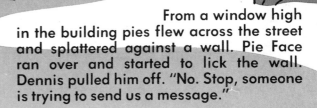

From a window high in the building pies flew across the street and splattered against a wall. Pie Face ran over and started to lick the wall. Dennis pulled him off. "No. Stop, someone is trying to send us a message."

Pie Face ran to the door and tried to gnaw his way into the factory. Gnasher had recovered his appetite by this time and gave him a hand. Soon they were in and running up the stairs to find Mr Crusty tied to a chair in the middle of the room.

He was still throwing pies out of the window. His message was finished now and all he was trying to do was hit passers by for his own amusement. He stopped when he saw his rescuers. "Saved! Someone has found me. I can go back to supplying Beanotown with my pies."

Dennis untied him without help from Pie Face or Gnasher, who were both deep in a pile of pies chomping wildly. "Who did this terrible thing to you, Mr Crusty, and why?"

Before he could answer, a woman appeared. "I did it. I'm Pie Face's Mum. Pie Face eats nothing but pies. I thought that if I could stop the supply of pies he would eat some of the things I cook — salads, soup, trifle, prawn cocktail and things like that."

Pie Face lifted his head from the pile of pies he was devouring. "Sorry, Mum. I could never let anything but a pie past my lips."

Mr Crusty thought about it for a moment. "I might just have a solution . . ."

And so it was that Mr Crusty began to make pies filled with salad, soup, trifle and prawn cocktail (No — not all in the one pie, stupid) just for Pie Face. They tasted foul, but Pie Face will eat anything in a pie case, so he was happy. Mr Crusty was happy because he didn't get tied up by Pie Face's Mum any more. Pie Face's Mum was happy because Pie Face ate her trifle, etc.

Dennis said he was only going to be happy if he could get the garden shed that Pie Face had destroyed replaced. Mr Crusty was happy to oblige. He baked a giant pie shell and put it in the place where the shed had been. It looks stupid and the next door neighbours hate it. But since Dennis's next door neighbour is Walter, he ended up happy too.

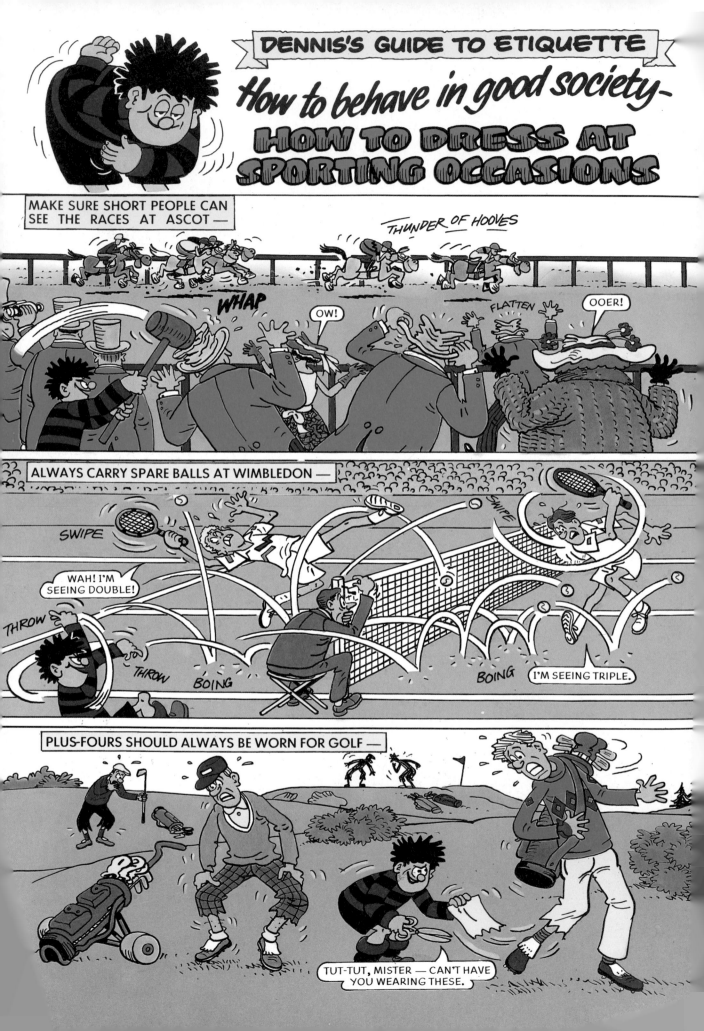

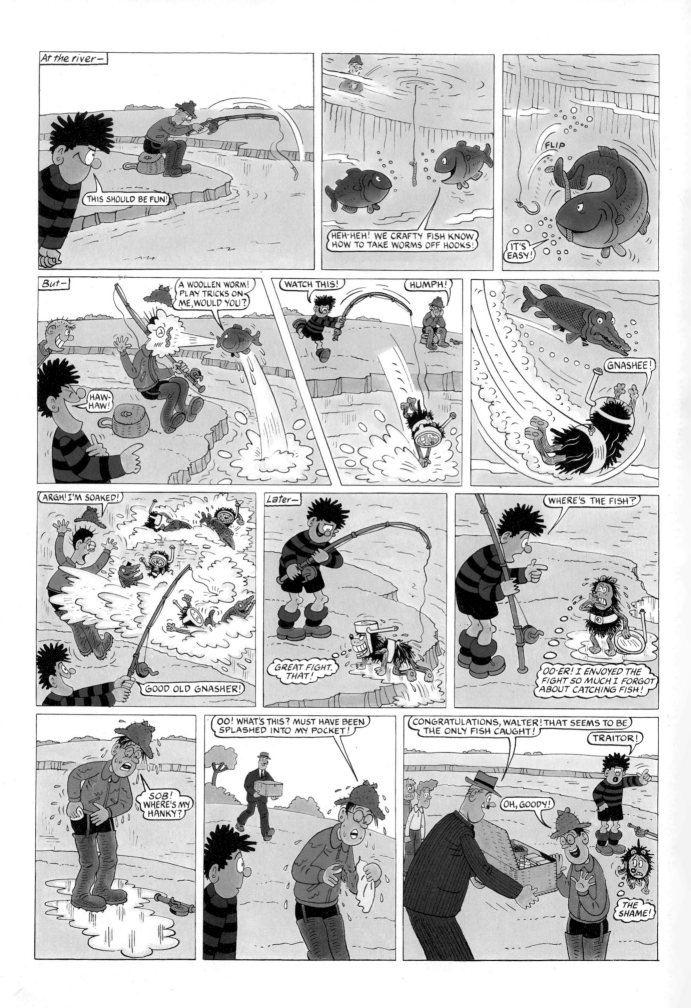

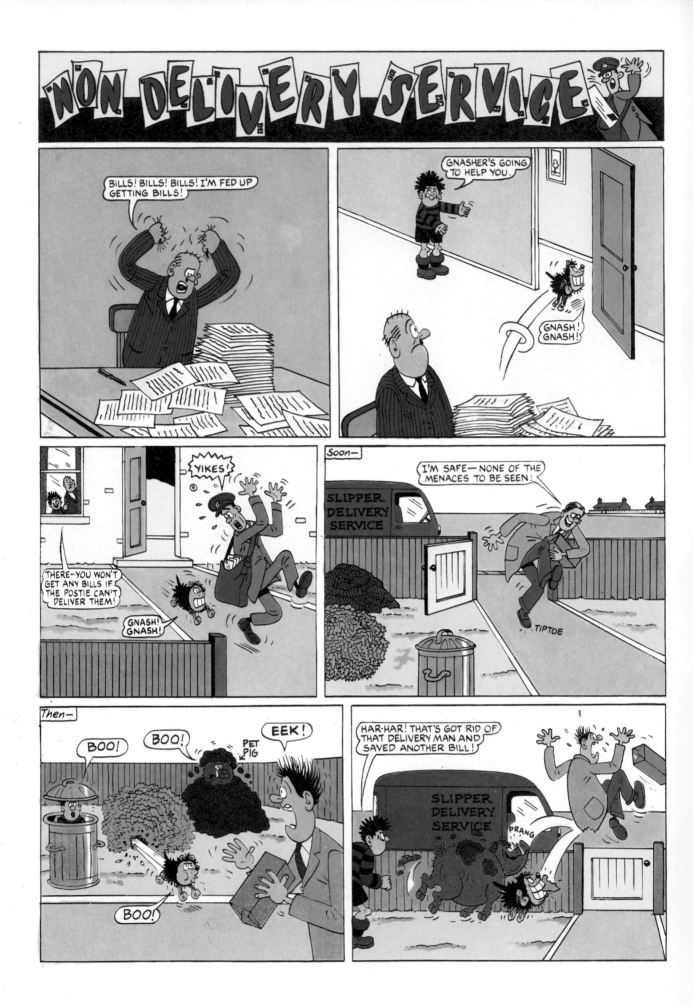

SPLAT the

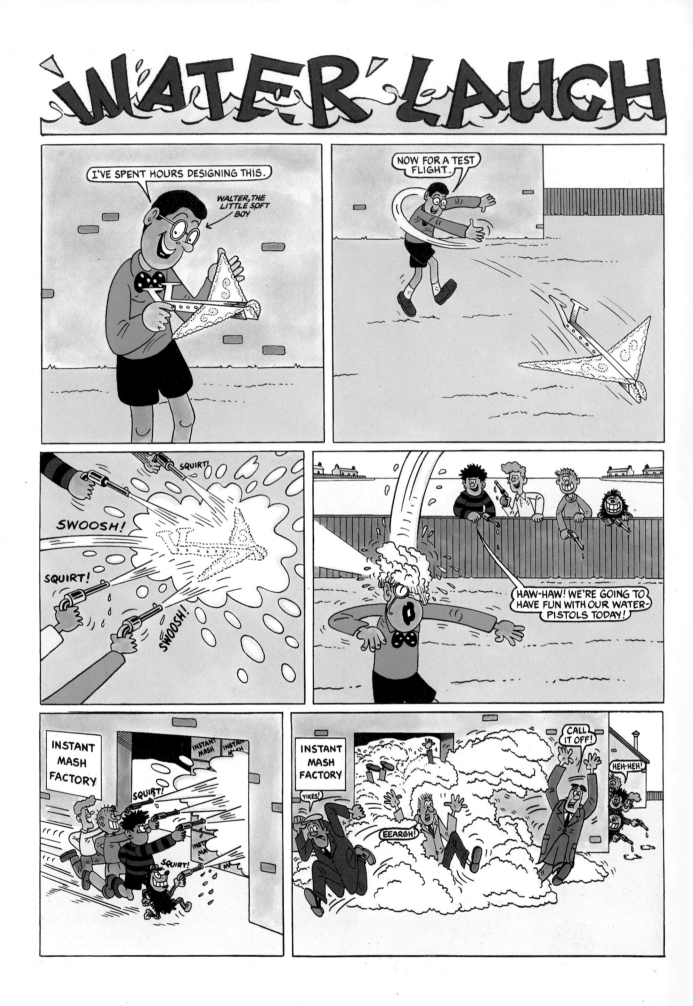

SIMON HILL, DERBY.

SAM MEACOCK, INVERNESS.

PAUL TRUMAN, TRURO CORNWALL.

NEIL HAMPTON, COLCHESTER ESSEX.

LIAM CURTIS, SALISBURY WILTSHIRE.